Mastering Social Media

A Step-by-Step Guide to Putting Your Business Online

Syd Bolton

Published by...

Personal Computer Museum
13 Alma Street
Brantford, Ontario, N3R 2G1
Canada

ISBN-13: 978-1480034730
ISBN-10: 1480034738

Contents

1. Introduction 3

2. Facebook..5

3. Twitter...15

4. Google Plus 23

5. YouTube...29

6. Developing and following a strategy..................35

7. Measuring Success.......................................41

8. Conclusion 45

Acknowledgements

The development of this book was born primarily out of a need to have an additional take away for those people who come to my business seminars. I'd like to thank Sue Loveless and Larry Voegtle of the Norfolk District Business Development Corporation for giving me the initial push. Thank you also goes to Trudy Belanco for believing in me from the beginning and starting me on a path to professional speaking that began decades ago. Finally, to all the local social media butterflies around me like Trevor Cherewka, Jamie Stephens, Robert Lavigne, and many others who constantly push me - in their own ways - to do better, be better, and communicate better through social media.

The cover of the book was designed by Azu Mendoza of Virtual Evolutions Design Studio. The photograph of me on the back of the book was taken by Greg McMillan.

Dedication

To Jennifer, who makes me think about social media in new and different ways.

Chapter 1: Introduction

It has become very clear that virtually every business that exists today can benefit from social media. In the past, consumers would turn to things like the *Yellow Pages* to get information about businesses by category and with the growth of the Internet and the World Wide Web, consumers now turn there as their number one choice for getting information on businesses. In fact, some estimates put consumers going to the web first at over 80% of the time.

Social Media adds additional elements to all of this. It allows us to find, with very little effort, what our friends and family think about various choices we make when selecting a business. It also adds the elements of a two way conversation between consumer and business (or business to business) that we have never had before.

The benefit of the "old way" is that it was pretty easy. Placing an ad or even getting a website designed for you is pretty easy. Creating a presence on social media is tougher because it's often a more direct reflection of the business – and ultimately you – that will require your input, time and creativity. It's not always easy if you don't know where to start and many questions will pop up for you along the way.

Facebook, while having great dominance in social media, is also the place where people have the most questions. Although the site is realitively easy to navigate there are a lot of hidden gems hidden within that can help you get even more success outside of the big sandbox that it has become.

This book will provide you the step by step instructions on creating an online presence, help you develop a strategy to keep it going and provide you the tools to get at the metrics to measure how you are doing. Doing something well is never easy, but this book will get you on the right path to real success using social media.

Chapter 2: Facebook

Facebook is by far the most popular social media website in North America. With over 800 million users, Facebook is the place to be. Statistics (from checkfacebook.com) tell us that the most popular segments of users are between the ages of 18-34, but that the other age segments keep going up. The break down by gender is that 55% of users are female (and of course the other 45% are male).

First Steps

If you are already on Facebook, you can jump to the next step: **Creating a Company Page.**

If you do not have an account on Facebook, you will need one to create a company page and administer it. It does not mean you have to become an active "Facebooker" or use the site as others do, but creating an administrative account is a must. Note that, in accordance with Facebook's terms of service, one person may have only one account.

NOTE: DO NOT create an account in the name of the business. For example, do not create a person called "BOBS PIZZA". Instead, create an account with your real name and then register a company page called "Bob's Pizza". It is a violation of Facebook's terms of service to create an account for anyone other than an actual person.

With your web browser, go to "www.facebook.com" and start the process by filling out the following form:

Note that it is possible to keep everything except your name as "Private" if you are concerned about others finding out your age or your e-mail address. Facebook's own articles on the topic are quite extensive, so visit the website below if you need help or guidance in setting up your privacy options.

Once your account is set up you are ready to create a company page.

Facebook Privacy URL:

http://www.facebook.com/help/privacy

Creating a Company Page

There are several different places and ways you can get to the "Create Page" section of Facebook. To be consistent and to make it easier for everyone, I recommend that you simply go to the "Search Box" at the top of the page when you are logged into Facebook. Type "create page" (the case doesn't matter). Click on the top choice, as shown below:

You will get a page with six choices:

Your choice will be between "Local Business or Place" and "Company, Organization or Institution". In most cases you will choose "Local Business or Place". Examples where you would choose "Company, Organization, or Institution" would be if you are a not-for-profit, or you are creating the "head office" of a franchise. In this step-by-step example we will choose "Local Business or Place".

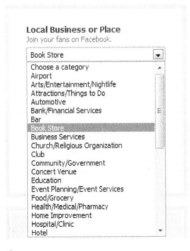

Step 1 is to choose a category. A drop down list will appear (shown here on the left) and you should choose the one that best describes your business. In this example, we'll select a Book Store.

After that, enter the name of your business, address, city, postal code, and phone number. You will also have to agree to "Facebook Pages Terms". You should read this, especially the part about "Promotions". Then click to agree.

Your page should look something like this:

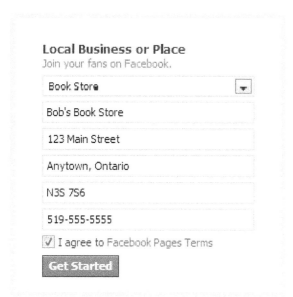

Just three major steps remain to getting your page online. First, you should choose a picture for your business profile. At this stage it will be handy to have a picture of the business that you want to use but if you don't you can always skip this step. You can also choose "Import From Website" if you don't have a picture on your computer handy. Keep in mind that this is only a last resort step and you should always try and upload an original, high resolution picture from your computer where possible.

This step looks like this:

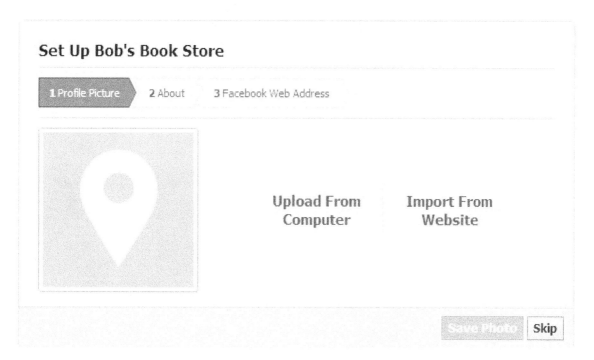

If you click on "Upload From Computer" you will be able to locate a picture (preferably a JPEG file) on your local computer and select it. If you don't have a picture available don't worry, just click on "Skip". If you are happy with your choice, select "Save Photo".

The next step is to create the "About" section of the page. Here you will provide a general description about your business and include links to your website and Twitter accounts (if applicable). It looks like this:

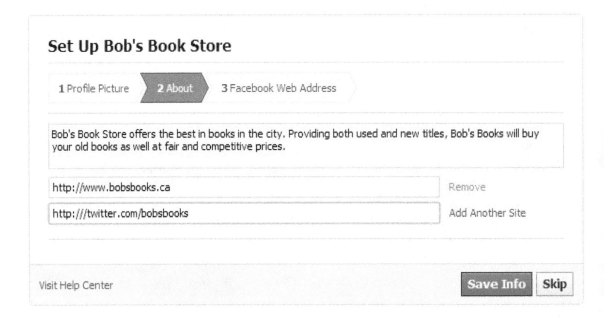

Just click in the appropriate box to enter information. Website links should always have the "http://" in front of them. This is an example of a completed entry:

Set Up Bob's Book Store

| 1 Profile Picture | 2 About | 3 Facebook Web Address |

Bob's Book Store offers the best in books in the city. Providing both used and new titles, Bob's Books will buy your old books as well at fair and competitive prices.

http://www.bobsbooks.ca   Remove

http:///twitter.com/bobsbooks   Add Another Site

Visit Help Center   Save Info   Skip

The last step is **very important**. This will determine your Facebook Web Address, something that you will use later on to promote your site. It can be almost as important as the domain name you have for your website (if applicable).

Facebook will make a suggestion for you based upon what the name of your business is, and what is available to be used. Here is an example:

Set Up Bob's Book Store

1 Profile Picture   2 About   **3 Facebook Web Address**

Choose a unique Facebook web address to make it easier for people to find your Page. We've made a suggestion below, but you can also choose your own. Once this is set, it can't be changed.

http://www.facebook.com/ BobsBookStore

Set Address   **Skip**

Unlike most other things that you put on your page, the Facebook address you use *cannot be changed* once it is set, so choose wisely.

After this step is complete, your page is ready to go! You can of course make additional changes. You will be taken to the page right away. One big difference between what you see (as an administrator) and what everyone else sees is the "Admin Panel". Before we get into that, there are a few other steps you should perform on your new page.

NOTE: At this stage, avoid clicking on the "Like" button for your new page. Doing so will draw attention to your page before it is ready for general consumption.

The rest of the steps are optional and can be done in any order.

Adding Your Hours

It is important for people to know when your business is open and you are available. Right near the basic information about your business (like the name and address) you will see an option to "Add Your Hours". If you haven't added a profile picture yet, you will also be prompted to do so.

Actually adding your hours is fairly simple. If you are open the same hours you can select to "Apply to

all days" after setting one day. You can also choose to say you are always open (for online businesses) or "No hours available".

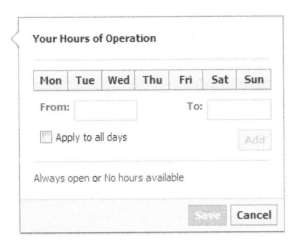

Adding a Cover

In addition to the profile picture, Facebook has something called a "Cover" that is a widescreen canvas that goes behind your profile picture.

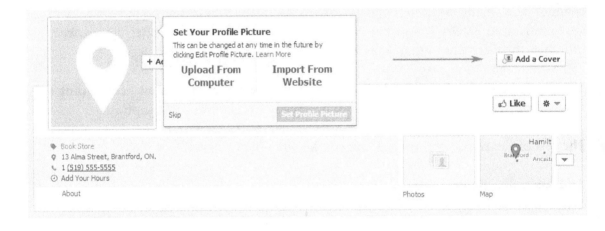

Covers are just pictures – but they are much wider than they are tall. Facebook will allow you to "crop" an existing picture to match its requirements.

For those more technically minded, you could choose to create a photo of the exact required dimension (851 pixels wide by 315 high). If you don't understand what that means, feel free to ignore it and just click on "Add a Cover" and select a picture from your computer to use as a cover image.

Here is an example of what a cover photo and profile picture might look like.

Personal Computer Museum
564 likes · 14 talking about this · 131 were here

✓ Liked   ✿ ▾

Profile Picture

The profile picture is "inset" in the bottom left corner of the cover. Facebook will scale down any photograph you provide into a 160 pixel by 160 pixel thumbnail. The minimum requirement for a photo you submit, however, must be at least 200 pixels in each dimension. The important thing to note, especially if you want to make sure that logos or other important details do not get chopped out of an image, is to make your profile pictures square in nature (in other words, pictures should have the same height and width for dimensions). While this is not a requirement, it will prevent any unexpected cropping of your photographs.

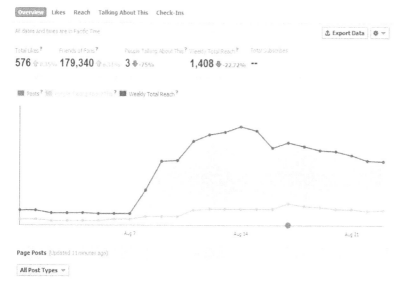

Insights

Once your page has received 30 "Likes" you can access Facebook insights. This information is very valuable and can help you determine what works for your page and what doesn't. When you go to your page, in the Admin panel simply click on "See All" in the Insights section.

By default, Insights will show you an "Overview" that provides you a wealth of information. The purple dots along the bottom will show you when you made a post on the page and from that, you can see what effect it has on your overall reach. Posting is the easiest way to get people to talk about your posts. The weekly total reach represents the number of unique people that have seen posts from your page.

Likes

Clicking on "Likes" gives you a very detailed breakdown of the people who like your page (and are therefore receiving your updates). It looks something like this:

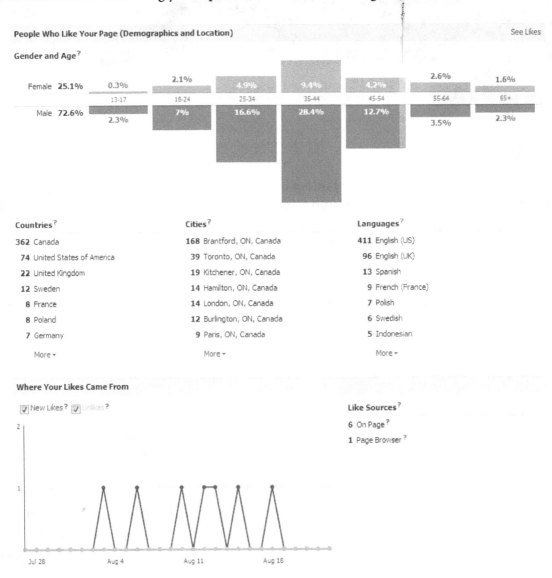

The breakdown of Male vs. Female should be the first thing that you analyze, followed by the age breakdown. In this example, the page insights are for a vintage technology related business so it makes sense that there are 72.6% male subscribers and that the bulk of those are between 25 and 54 years of age. If these demographics do not match your business target market, you may not be reaching the right people.

The next step is to look at the breakdown by Countries, Cities, and Languages. Again, these should make sense for your actual business demographics. If they don't, you need to work at reaching the right people. Social media is great at reaching out to larger audiences, but it can also lead to ineffective broadcasts. Use these insights to make sure you are on track.

Reach, Talking About This, Check-Ins

The other tabs provide additional information about your page. As time permits, you should check these out as well because they can also provide useful additional information.

Getting Help and Advanced Features

In the upper right section of the Insights panel you will see an option to Export the Data. You can choose the date range and then choose to export the data directly to Microsoft Excel format or the more generic CSV (Comma Separate Values) format that will work with virtually any spreadsheet or text editor. Exporting the data will allow you to create your own custom charts and graphs if you need to do so for a report for example.

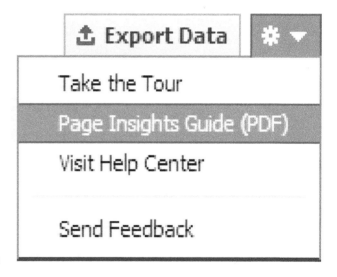

The drop down menu here also allows you to "Take the Tour" of the features included with Insight, or you can even download the "Page Insights Guide" which is a PDF file that you can print and read offline to understand all of the features offered in Insights. There are many things buried under the hood that could be useful to understanding who is visiting your page, what your reach is, and how your posts are affecting that reach. From this, you should be able to draw some conclusive conclusions.

These are advanced features that can really help you understand the visitors you are getting to your page.

Narrowing Down the Insights

By default, the Insights default to "All Post Types". If you want to narrow it down, click on the drop down and choose from the choices available. This will allow you to see what is more effective – your posts, your photos and so on. Use this breakdown to determine what is working best for you.

Understanding what type of post works best for you over time will help you focus on what is best. Some businesses benefit from great photos being posted, others receive better response from posts that include specials or coupons.

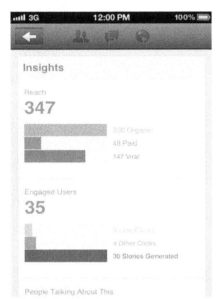

iPhone App

In addition to the regular "Facebook" app that you might be using on your smart phone, there is an iPhone app called "*Facebook Pages Manager*". This app is specifically designed to let you manage your business pages and do most of what you can do on the computer. It even allows you access to Insights and other advanced features. If you spend more time on your phone than in front of a computer, this could be the app for you. This is a free download in the App Store (just search for "Facebook Pages Manager"). It is also usually shown on the admin panel of your page. The diagram on the left shows you an example of what the app looks like.

Buying Ads on Facebook

There is a button that will show up when you are looking at your page from time to time that says "Promote Your Page". This is an option for you to purchase ads that will appear on the right hand side of people's pages. Facebook allows you to choose the demographics of the people seeing your ads very carefully (such as age, sex, and interests). This is an entirely separate topic and will not be covered further here, but you should be aware of its existence.

Conclusion

You should now have your Facebook page setup. Check the section on building a strategy to get more "likes" on your page.

Chapter 3: Twitter

Twitter is probably the most misunderstood of the Social Media tools out there. With over 500 million users, however, it is a force to be reckoned with. One of the recent taglines for Twitter is "Find out what's happening, right now, with the people and organizations you care about". There is a definite immediacy to Twitter.

More so than the other social networks I find there is a polarization with Twitter. There are those that "get it" and those that don't. It seems like you are all in or you just ignore it.

Previously, when describing the difference between Twitter and Facebook I would describe Twitter as a radio station that anyone can tune into and Facebook as your private puppet theater that you bring only your friends into. When Facebook added the ability for anyone to "Like" a page they essentially became more of a broadcast medium like Twitter.

People that tend to get "lost" in social media tend to enjoy Twitter better. Not only are the messages shorter, but website links and photos are optional and aren't put in your face when you are looking at the feed. For some people, this makes all of the difference.

Some businesses I deal with stick primarily with Facebook, while others use Twitter. I think that it's important to be on both although I would recommend that you adjust your efforts based upon your audience. In time, you will know which one feels "better" for your business. At the same time, you don't want to ignore those that choose one of the social media giants over the other over personal preference.

First Steps

If you are already registered on Twitter, you can jump to the section called "Customizing your Twitter Account".

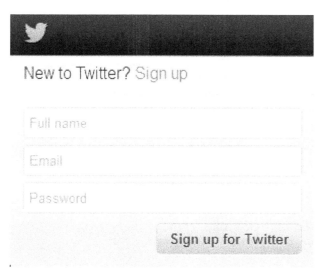

Point your browser to twitter.com. You should see an option to sign up, similar to this.

At this point you are probably wondering if you should use your real name or the name of the business. According to the terms of service, you are supposed to use your real name even though some people don't. There are many arguments as to why you should stick with your real name (but at the same time use it to promote your business). I'll give you a few examples.

The first reason to do so is to establish yourself as a professional who is knowledgeable on one or more topics (the most important being your business and whatever service and/or products that it sells). Secondly, you will attract more followers because it has been proven that people are more likely to follow a person over a brand. Finally, if you do decide to do something different in the future you will not have to drop or change your Twitter account.

The next step will have you fill out just a few more things. Your name and e-mail address will automatically transfer to this screen. Note that your name is checked to ensure it's a real name, and your password will be checked to make sure it is secure. If all of that is a go, you will next have to choose a username. This is of course very important and could be a chance for you to incorporate the name of the business or a brand.

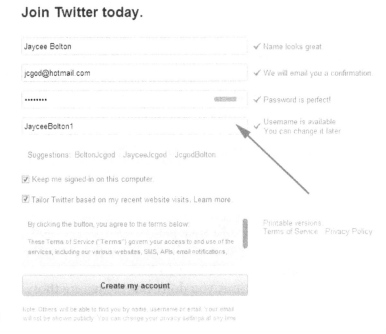

Twitter will automatically choose an available username for you based upon your name. You are free to change it later. In realtime, Twitter will check the availability of that username and let you know if you can use it or not.

Once you have all green checkmarks and have read the terms of service (okay, I know you probably won't read the whole thing) click on "Create my account".

Before you actually continue with the next step, you should go to your e-mail address and confirm your account. This will help keep your account active and also ensure that you can receive e-mails from the system in case problems arise in the future. The e-mail will have a subject similar to "**Confirm your Twitter account, Username**". If you don't see the e-mail within a few minutes, make sure you check your SPAM or JUNK folders for the message.

Once this step is complete, you will be taken to the *Twitter Teacher* who takes you step by step through the process of getting your account going.

Once you are ready to continue, simply click on "Next" and you can start to setup the rest of your account. Since Twitter is a two-way communication system, the system encourages you to "listen" before you "talk". Like Facebook, Twitter has a news feed that shows you the "tweets" (messages) from others in chronological order. For the first five people you follow, Twitter recommends those that already have a lot of followers (usually celebrities). This step looks something like this:

Called "Build your timeline", this step is actually optional (just click on "Skip this step" in the bottom left corner). I would recommend that you at least follow a feel people to understand how they use Twitter, so select the first five people by clicking on "Follow". Remember, you can always unfollow them later.

The next step is "See who's here" and shows you people that are on Twitter in various categories (such as Music, Sports, and Entertainment). It also shows you a preview of the five people you chose during the last step. Pick five more people (or choose to "Skip this step") to move on.

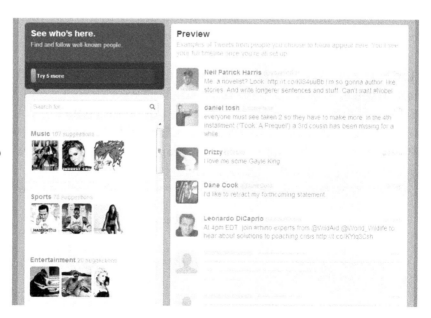

Next, you'll want to "Find people you know". This is where Twitter can actually go through your existing contacts and find out which ones have Twitter accounts already and you can choose to follow those individuals if you wish. If the e-mail address you have entered is a major web-based email (such as Hotmail, Gmail, Yahoo Mail, etc) then you can just give Twitter your username and password to have it securely check your contacts with its internal database. This step is safe and doesn't send notices to people, it just uses the information to present you with a list of people that are already on Twitter. It's simply a convenience. If you feel uncomfortable at all, once again you can "Skip this step".

"Add character" gets to the first stage of where you can start branding and adding true personalization to your account. You are going to want to upload an image (picture) to go along with your account. This is an important step and you should think about whether you want to include a picture of yourself, your business, or even an individual product (or service). At this point, I'll let you decide what is best for you because the answer here depends on a number of factors. Changing the image is very easy, so if you decide to use a picture of a product for example, consider changing it from time to time to keep it fresh.

The only technical restriction on this is that pictures must be 700 kilobytes in size or less. If you are not technically oriented, don't worry about it and just try to upload your picture. If the system rejects it, try using a different picture. If you are still having trouble, find the nearest teenager to assist you. Okay, all kidding aside, if you are not great with Photoshop or other photo editing programs, you can use the website "Pic Resize" to make your photos smaller. It's free and easy to use.

Pic Resize URL:

http://www.picresize.com

At this point, your Twitter account setup is complete. On the left side you will see how manypeople you are following, how many tweets you have sent out, and how many people are following you. You can also post a message here as well.

The next box continues to give you recommendations on who you should follow. The last box shows you what topics are "trending", which simply means the topics people are talking about the most. You will need to learn how to use **hash tags** (#) to indicate specific subject matter to more effectively categorize your tweets.

Customizing your Twitter Account

In addition to having a great profile picture on your account, you can also customize the look and feel of your page when visitors come and look. Although many people use Twitter with mobile phones, web visitors get additional graphics and color schemes that can make your Twitter page stand out.

By default, Twitter gives you a a basic theme that is blue in nature with clouds in the background.

To make changes, click on the "Cog wheel" on the top row. Select "Settings" from the menu.

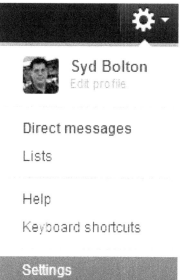

You should take note at this point that if you ever want to change your username, you can do it from the settings menu and this is also the place where you can change preferences like your primary language and the time zone. You can also choose to add your location to your tweets. Please use this option carefully.

There is also an option here called "Protect my Tweets" which allows you to control who receives your tweets. Do not use this option unless you have a very specific reason to do so. Limiting your tweets means you limit the people you can reach out to. One possible use of protecting your tweets could be using a special twitter account to communicate to a closed group or sales team, for example.

On the left hand side of the screen you will see an option to change a number of things. The one that is probably most important to the branding of your business is the one marked "Design".

Select "Design" and you will be given the option of choose a premade theme or customizing the look and feel of your page.

If you are in a hurry, or don't have any special graphics made up to support your Twitter account, the premade

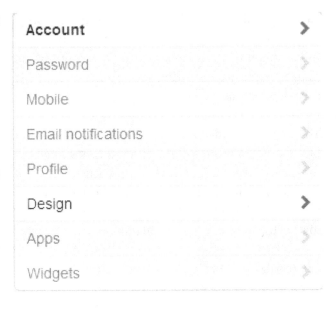

themes can work. You should at least change from the default one, since more people have that one than any other.

When it comes to custom graphics that will really make your account stand out there are two sections you can change - the "Header" and the 'Background". You can also just modify the background color and the link color.

Changing the Header

The header is the area where your profile picture and bio appear. Normally, this has a white background but you can replace this with an image (JPEG). The recommended dimension for this part is 1200 pixels across by 600 down. The file size can be a maximum of 5 megabytes, which is plenty large enough.

The dimensions of the image allow for scaling appropriately on most devices. Remember, people use Twitter on computers, tablets, and phones, all of which have varied sizes.

The above image is an example of what a custom header could look like. Because text (your name and bio) is placed on top of the header you should avoid using logos or text that are important to be obscured. In the above example, there is text on the boxes but it is not important enough to worry about the text being on top.

Changing the Background

The background is probably more important to change than the header because you easily include your logo, address of your business and virtually anything else that you want on your page. This is where proper branding can really be put to good use. If you are not technically savvy with a photo editing program (such as Photoshop or PaintShop Pro) you may have to get someone to help you with this. If you are looking for a good free editor, I would recommend GIMP (www.gimp.org).

Changing the background itself is as easy as clicking on "Change Background" but requires a bunch of forethought to get it just right. Also, there is a physical limit of only 800K for the image itself.

From a technical perspective, the image should be 1600 pixels across by 1200 high. You can use smaller images and allow them to "tile" but I would not recommend this because it can produce undesired results on certain screen sizes. Make sure the option to "Tile background" is turned off.

Every screen out there is different so your results may vary with what you put together. In the future, it is likely that screen resolutions will continue to get bigger. For now, use the recommended 1600 by 1200 and keep your business information strictly to the left side. This example will illustrate.

This background contains business information on the left hand side. The "T" in the bottom right corner is an extra element but will actually not be seen on all screens.

It is important not to include anything important on the right hand side as it is likely to get obscured by the tweets themselves.

I also chose to change the background color to match the dominant green in the picture. Using tools included in the photo editing software, I was able to determine that this green had a value of #119349. I plunked this number into the design settings for an even more attractive page. The combined result looks like this:

As you can see, the logo and branding are clearly visible on the left, but the "T" logo on the right is not visible (only the very top is showing).

While adding a custom header and background aren't critical to success with Twitter, they do add an element of professionalism to your account.

Chapter 4: Google Plus

When Google Plus was launched on June 28, 2011 it was met with a lot of skepticism. Google had tried "social" before without much success, and people were not sure how much better Google Plus would be.

Since then, there have been at least 400 million users registered on the service but this can be a little misleading. Essentially, anyone signing up for a GMail account (gmail.com) automatically gets added to the Google Plus system. Estimates put active users at approximately 100 million, or 25% of the registered user base.

Google Plus adoption has been much slower than either Facebook or Twitter and in terms of priority you should probably place it third or fourth on your list of "to dos". Having said that, some users have been very successful at finding an audience with Google Plus and a lot of it could have to do with who your target market is.

For example, Facebook is occupied by more men than women and contains a more even and general distribution of interests. According to socialstatistics.com, Google Plus currently has approximately 70% male users and only 30% female users. This skewed ratio can be useful in deciding how much time and effort to put into your Google Plus account.

First Steps

If you already have a GMail account then you already have Google Plus, so jump forward to the section marked "Setting up a Google Plus Business Page".

Point your browser to http://plus.google.com. You will be asked to sign in and if you don't have an account, click on "Sign Up". Something like this will appear:

Fill everything out and remember that this particular account will be your personal one. You will learn how to create a business page in the next section.

After you have entered the basics, you will will be taken to the next step.

The next step will show your name and allow you to add a profile photo. You can skip this step if you wish, at which point you will be allowed to continue to Google+. You will also receive an e-mail asking you to confirm your account.

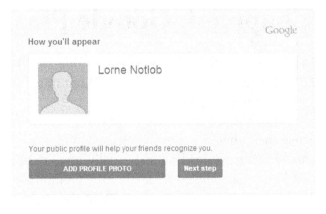

When you first get into Google Plus you will be asked if you want to follow interesting people and pages. This allows you to receive updates and shared links from others. The system gives you suggestions and you should also consider at this point following other businesses and people you know.

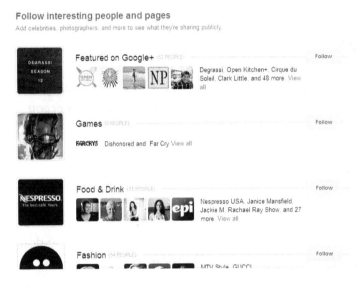

The final step (labelled "Be Awesome") encourages you to keep your image fresh. If you haven't already added a photo to your profile, now is the time to do so. This page will even activate a web camera to snap a current photo of you (if you have one attached of course) or you can upload an image if you skipped that step previously.

It will also ask you about where you work at, where you have gone to school and where you live. These items are all publically visible at the time you add them, so please consider this if you are concerned about privacy.

Once you are all done simply click on the "Finish" button and you will be ready to create a business page.

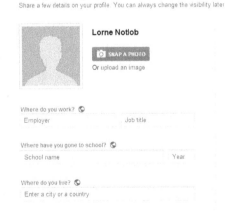

Setting up a Google Plus Business Page

Google Plus uses a menu bar that goes along the left side of your browser. By default, the option for managing pages is not visible. If you look at the bar on the left you will notice at the bottom an option for "More". When you hover over this you will see an option for "Pages".

NOTE: It is possible that the "Pages" icon, shown here on the right, is already in the menu. This happens if you have already created a page.

After you have clicked on the "Pages" icon you will be presented with a list of pages you have - and it also gives you the ability to create a new one. It looks something like this:

Simply click on "Create new page" to get started.

Much like Facebook Pages, you must now pick a category for your business page. One of the main differences is that the "Local Business or Place" is tied to existing Google databases. If your business is already on Google Local, it will find it and tie it in. If it's not, you should consider adding your business to the database. It helps with searches tremendously.

If your business does not have a physical presence or would not been found in a business database with a telephone number associated with it, choose "Company, Institution, or Oranization". Otherwise, select "Local Business or Place". Obviously if you want to promote a product or brand or have a sports group choose the appropriate button.

In our example, we'll choose "Local Place or Business" and make sure the country field is set correctly. After that, enter in the phone number of your business to see if Google has information available on your business.

If it doesn't, you will have to fill in various fields manually. If it knows about your business it will fill out as many of the fields as possible.

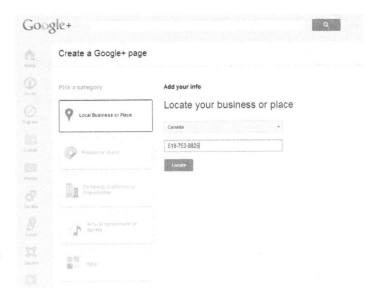

If your business is found, click on it. If it is not you can always "Add your business to Google". This is a good practice to do at this point if it is not done. The specific steps are beyond the scope of this book, but it is fairly straightforward and has many other benefits beyond just Google Plus.

Once the business is selected properly you can move on to changing your profile.

At this point you will want to have a photo for your business profile. The dimensions of the final photo are 256 pixels by 256 pixels. It is best to have one sized to this automatically, but Google will do it for you if you don't have that type of photo available.

It is most important to note that the picture should be the same dimensions high as it is wide. Landscape photos will end up getting cropped.

Customize your page's public profile

Profile basics

These are just the basics of your page's profile. You can fill out a complete profile later.

PROFILE PHOTO

Give your page some personality with an icon, brand, or profile photo.

The image you choose will represent you when you post, leave comments, or interact with other people and pages on Google+!

Set profile photo

Continue »

©2012 Google - Terms - Privacy

After choosing a picture from your computer's hard drive, it will appear on the screen.

If you are not happy with it, you can change it. If you are happy, you can simply click on "Continue" to go to the next step.

At this point, your page is done with the basics attached. You will now be asked if you want to promote the page to your personal "circles". Circles are Google's way of controlling privacy. You literally have social circles that can include friends, family, or anything you like.

You can skip this step if you want, but if you are ready to get the word out right away you should share away.

Once you click on "Share on Google+" you will be asked to confirm which of your circles will see it. Since you are most likely trying to spread the word to as many people as possible you should leave the default setting to "Public".

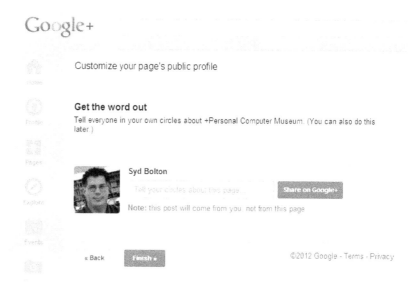

Customize your page's public profile

Get the word out

Tell everyone in your own circles about +Personal Computer Museum. (You can also do this later.)

Syd Bolton

Tell your circles about this page...

Share on Google+

Note: this post will come from you, not from this page

« Back   Finish »

©2012 Google - Terms - Privacy

It is also possible to add specific people to the share if you want to make sure they take note of it.

Look over what you are saying carefully. Having spelling and grammar mistakes in posts like this can make a big difference to certain target markets. Once you are happy that everything looks good you can just click on "Share" to send the news out.

Now that your page is setup, you are going to need to know how to make changes to it and create a buzz for your business. Simply click on the "Pages" icon on the Google Plus menu (which may now be docked into the menu itself) and you will now notice that your page is available.

If you hover over this option you will see the "Settings" and "Managers" choices. The settings will allow you to make changes to things like the profile picture and the managers option is great to allow co-workers or employees access to the page to make changes. This takes the burden of updating off of you, and if applicable, will make your life easier.

Clicking on "Switch to this page" will now take you to your page and any subsequent posts that you do (and sharing of pictures, and videos for example) will all appear under your business page.

Chapter 5: YouTube

Traditionally, YouTube is not considered a social media website. The tagline "Broadcast Yourself" sums up the idea behind the site. You upload videos that you create and share them with others. Making your own television station is now possible!

Of course, it's never that easy. Or is it? Creating videos can be a very involved and expensive process. Videos that are on YouTube range from zero budget to millions of dollars. Surprisingly, they both have value at the end of the day.

If you don't have a video camera (don't forget, most smart phones can double as video cameras too) or, more importantly, you have no idea on how to edit videos please don't stop reading! I'll share with you tips on how anyone can create a video using only photographs in just a few easy steps.

There are a couple of good reasons why you should have a presence on YouTube. First of all, YouTube is a Google property. That means that all of the descriptions and videos are melded together with Google search results. Google likes to present users with search results that include both websites and videos on its site. Secondly, being the third most popular website in the world means that there are literally millions of people searching for and sharing videos. Your video could even go viral, being potentially viewed by millions of people.

First Steps

If you already have a YouTube account, please jump forward to the section titled "Making Your Business Video". Did you know that if you already have a Google account (say for GMail or Google Plus) then you already also have a YouTube account. Otherwise, the setup is the same as it is for Google Plus.

Just fill out your name and if you want to use a username connected to your business you can do so at this time. Remember, many common names will already be gone.

29

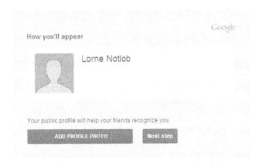

Although it's optional, you should really try and add a profile photo. This will always make yoru profile look better, complete and professional.

That's really all you need to do with YouTube. You can also add the URL (Uniform Resource Locator) - also known as a web address - of your business to your profile and a bio. That's it.

Making Your Business Video

Obviously if you have a video camera and the ability to edit said video, you can make your own videos fairly easily. If you don't, however, fear not! There are a number of choices available to you.

Using Your Smartphone

Smartphones such as the iPhone, BlackBerry and (most) Android phones offer the ability to use the built in camera for video recording. Some of the phones (the iPhone in particular) also offer apps that will allow you to edit the video right on the phone. Once you have a video shot, you can upload it directly to your YouTube account. How this is accomplished varies from phone to phone, so please make sure you read the instructions to know how to finish this step.

The most important thing to remember about creating an actual video for your business is having good lighting and good sound. These are the two areas that make videos look more amateur.

Making a Video From Pictures

So you don't have a video camera, or you are not comfortable with it. It's not a problem. If you have a good collection of photos from your business or product, that's all you need to create a great video.

The first thing you need to do is make a plan for what you want your video to be. If you are launching a new product or business, you probably have a number of pictures from the event or the product itself. If you can imagine putting together a slide show of all of these pictures (to music) then you know what you need to do.

First Steps

The first thing you should do for your project is create a folder in your computer to hold the photographs. Even if they are already somewhere, you want to copy the photos to this new folder and keep your original photos untouched. Once that is done, you need to put the photos in order.

Different computer operating systems will change the order of files in different ways, but most will default to showing your files in alphabetical order. Therefore, you should rename each of the photos in such a way that they will be in the order you desire. For example, you should put a prefix followed by the photo number. It is important, if you have more than 9 pictures, that you number them with two digits. For example, your first photo could be renamed "PHOTO-01", and the second one called "PHOTO-02". This would allow for 99 photos to be ordered correctly.

Once your photos are all in the folder and are in the order that you are happy with, you are almost ready to make your video!

Picking The Music

If you plan on sharing your video slideshow on a public website like YouTube, you are advised to use royalty free music. It is possible to use someone else's commercial music, but there are a number of problems with doing this. In the worst case, you will be asked to remove your content. In the best case, the song will be recognized and a link will be added for the user to download the song through a service like iTunes. When this happens, any potential chance you have of making money on the video will be removed from you, ads can be added and the revenues from those ads will be given to the music publishing company.

There are many choices when it comes to music you will be allowed to use. A website like http://www.smartsound.com offers some completely free music you can use legally, or some very low cost options where you pay a small one time fee and then are free to use the music from there on out.

Making the Video

On the Windows platform, Microsoft has a product called "Windows Live Movie Maker". It's a free product that is part of the "Windows Live Essentials" pack that is very easy to use and even offers built-in YouTube intregration. Once you have your photos and music, you are ready to go!

On your computer, Explore to where your photos are and select all of them (either with the mouse or by pressing CTRL-A). Once selected, you can drag them right into Movie Maker in the pane on the right.

Once your photos are in Movie Maker they will look something like this.

Adding the music is very simple. Just click on "Add Music" at the top and navigate to where the music you have is located. The music can be in common audio formats such as MP3 or WAV (wave).

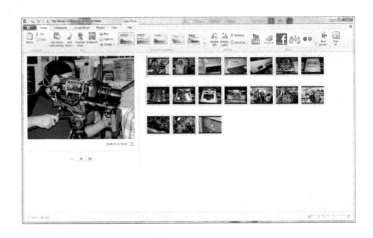

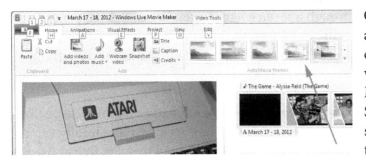

Once you have pictures and audio added to your project, you can use a nice feature included with Windows Live Movie Maker called "Auto Movie". Shown here with the arrow, you simply click on one of these and the program will add a title, end credits, transistions between the photos and automatically time it all out so that the photos are timed out to transition perfectly to the end of the music.

Now, just edit your title and ending credits/statement and you are done your video! Make sure you save at this point.

Sharing on YouTube

By simply clicking on the YouTube bottom at the top, you can share your video with the world. The first question you will be asked is about the resolution. Use 1440x1080, as this is the best.

You will be required to sign in to Windows Live first (if you don't have an account, such as a Live or Hotmail account, signing up is free and easy) and then you will need to sign into YouTube. You can set certain options including the TITLE and the DESCRIPTION which are the most important.

When adding your title, keep in mind what people would search for in order to find your product. If you are not sure the best title and description, try asking a friend to help. Input from someone not as close to your business can be very helpful.

That's all there is to it!

Making a Video Slide Show on the Mac

There are many different solutions to making a video slideshow out of pictures on the Mac. The least expensive is to use the built in iMovie software and follow the steps at Instrucables on how to do it.

Instructables URL:

http://www.instructables.com/id/How-to-make-a-video-slide-show-with-iMovie/

Animoto

If you are just not very technically inclined and the instructions for Movie Maker or iMovie scare the heck out of you, perhaps Animoto is the choice for you. A web based solution, Animoto allows you to upload your photos to its server and the cleverly written software will produce an animated slideshow for you that actually moves and goes to the beat of the chosen song (licensing already included).

Although it works amazingly well, the free version limits you to only 30 seconds per video, so you may need to pay for a subscription. Also, if you want any titles in the movie itself, you will have to use a photo editing program to create them as if they were a picture.

Other than that, it's a great service for those that don't have any other choices and the results are truly professional. Give it a try and see what what you think.

Conclusion

No matter how you make your video, adding it to YouTube can drive business to your website. Don't forget the following points:

• Include important keywords in your title that will make it easy for people to find your video
• Do not forget to include the URL (web address) of your website in the video. This will allow people a larger place to go to find out more information

So remember, the next time someone says you should add a video you can't say you don't have any video!

Chapter 6: Developing and following a strategy

Now that you have setup your social media account(s) you need to develop a strategy to follow. Creating the accounts are not enough, you must actually do something with them. This is where most people fail, so please pay close attention to the following suggestions.

First Steps

The most important part of developing a Social Media Strategy (SMS) is writing everything down. So, start up your word processor and create the headings "Facebook", "Twitter", "Google Plus", "YouTube" and "Web". Of course, leave out any headings that don't apply to you.

For each section, create a subtitles marked "Strategy & Goals", "Frequency", "Ideas", and "Successful Interactions". So the first part should look something like this:

Facebook

Strategy & Goals

Frequency

Ideas

Successful Interactions

Once you have created these sections for each item you are ready to start filling in the blanks. Remember the golden rule:

"Your Social Media Strategy is Always a Work In Progress"

Once you "complete" the document you should be going back to it constantly and make changes and adjustments to it.

Strategy & Goals

Your strategy and goals will depend entirely on the type of business you have. I can only offer you so much guidance in this area, and the rest must come from your understanding of your own business.

Your strategy should be a mixture of promotional ideas, frequency, and delivering value to your customers. Some important things to keep in mind:

"Study the practices of successful social media gurus"

Look closely at what people with a large number of friends on Facebook or a large following on Twitter are doing.

"Find your story - create a buzz around your business"

This is a tough one, but nobody can answer it better than you. Think about your business, and what is unique about it. Find a way to build a story around it and share it around the world.

Example: The Personal Computer Museum is a not-for-profit museum, presently the only interactive computer museum in all of Canada. However, in order to get the word out special projects have been initiated to draw attention to the museum. In late 2008 I came up with the idea of combining the latest hottest thing (Twitter) with one of the oldest things we have at the museum - a Commodore VIC-20. I developed the software to make it happen and in February 2009 the museum made history by having the VIC-20 tweet. The story was picked up by major outlets including the CBC, CNet news, and more. In fact if you search Google for the expression "VIC-20 on twitter", there are over 31 million results. They may not all be about this project, but a surprising number are. The story was covered in multiple languages by multiple outlets. The Twitter account "@vintagepc" was created just for this story (people were told to follow the account to be a part of history and see the first tweet ever from a VIC-20) and it quickly sprang to over 1,500 followers. Presently, there are over 2,500 followers on this account.

Frequency

This is a tricky question, and one of the most common ones. How often should you be posting? There is one golden rule with frequency always applies:

"Only post something when you have something important to say"

Some of you may feel you have something important to say all of the time, however, keep in mind that you must allow time for posts to be seen by the majority of your audience. Never post more than once an hour. If you are worried that you don't have enough to say, you should be posting at least once a week. Stuck for what to say?

"Make a list of things you want to say when you think of them"

Put them in your "Ideas" section and go to the list when you need to post something and aren't sure what to say.

"Make sure you post something at least once a week, preferably two or three times"

This will keep your audience engaged. If you post too much, you will subject your audience to social media fatigue. There is no straight answer on frequency, but your experience over time will you what is best for your business and for your audience.

"Time of day is important - pay attention to when your customers are most active"

Keeping in mind your target audience, choosing the time(s) of day that you will post can be very important. For example, if you are targeting mothers you should choose a time of day either mid morning or mid afternoon. These are, most commonly, down times where a mother might have a few spare moments to go on social media. Mornings will be filled with getting children to school and anytime after 3:00 PM can be lost to those picking up children from school. This is a broad example, but really think about who you are trying to reach and then make decisions about what time of day is best.

"Create an automatic reminder for social media postings"

If you find you are not posting frequently enough, create a reminder in your smart phone or on your computer with Outlook or another piece of software that can assist you with reminders. That way, even if you forget, your computer won't!

Ideas

The ideas section of your SMS should include ideas for future postings, and ideas for getting more engagement. In the case of Facebook, that means more "Likes". In the case of Twitter, that means more "Followers". It should include helpful hints that center around your business. A lot of "Did you know?" kind of ideas. For example, if you have a Pizza business you might have something like the following (please note, this is just an example and the facts and figures shown are not necessarily accurate):

1. Did you know that October is National Pizza month? It was first designated this in 1987.
2. Domino's Pizza is the world leader in delivery with 5,500 stores in 46 international markets.
3. Each year the largest pizza trade show, Pizza Expo takes place in Las Vegas, Nevada.

In this case, these are trivia items. They serve no real purpose other than to be interesting and educational. You should mix these with offers specific to your business. Continuing with the pizza theme, some of those might include:

1. Receive 10% off your pizza order by calling now and use the code "PizzaTweet1". Call 519-555-ZAAA

2. Tuesdays are Two for One. Order any regularly priced pizza today only and receive a second pizza of equal or lesser value for free! 519-555-ZAAA.

People, by nature, are lazy. If you notice I have included the phone number in each of the above statements because even though your page may have the phone number clearly listed having it right there in front makes it even easier and *removes a barrier* that some people may have when considering a *call to action*.

"In your business, identify all the barriers that may cause people not to take action"

Once you have identified the barriers, it's far easier to remove them for people in many cases or at least make them less of a barrier. This will make you successful.

Some of your ideas should revolve around increase engagement with your social media. In this case of Facebook, this means attracting more people to 'Like' your page. Do not obsess too much about the number of likes you have. There are a number of ways to achieve additional likes but they are not necessarily people truly interested in your business, so what is the point? Some people look at it as a vanity number but what you want are truly engaged people that will conduct business with you and share what you are doing with others. This, in the long run, will increase business.

Here are some ideas on how to increase your followers or 'Likers':

1. Hold contests. Give away product, services, or gift certificates if people 'Like' or follow you, but don't forget those already loyal to you. Example "When we reach 500 followers on Twitter, we'll draw for a prize of everyone following of X".

2. On Facebook, post personal status updates that make reference to your business page by including the "@" symbol in front. For example, I could type "We are open this Saturday at the @Personal Computer Museum". This would then show the Personal Computer Museum page as a link that people can click on and like.

3. Leverage traditional media - remind people on radio, print or television advertising that you can "Find us on Twitter" or "Find us on Facebook".

4. Involve related groups. There are many special interest groups on Facebook and all throughout the internet (sometimes these are called Bulletin Boards). Involve those groups related by posting information about your business, but don't necessarily make it an ad. Example: The Personal Computer Museum ran a Tetris Tournament in 2008. I contacted the administrator of a "Tetris Fan Page" with over 5,000 people in it and asked her if it was okay that I posted about the tournament on the page. She agreed (and even

helped promote it on her personal page) and this brought additional attention to the museum itself.

5. Cross promote. Pump your Facebook page on Twitter and vice versa. Post links to your Facebook page on Google Plus and mention to your Twitter followers that you can see updates on Google Plus.

6. Get your webmaster to include a Facebook "Like" box on your website, and also include links to your Twitter and/or Google Plus accounts too.

7. Engage people by taking pictures at your store or at special events, and then ask everyone to "Tag" themselves in the photos. This way, all of *their* friends will see *your* pictures, leading to more interaction.

8. If you have a newsletter or e-mail blast, use it to promote your social media offerings.

9. Make sure you include references to all social media accounts on your business cards, brochures and other printed materials. It takes only the right person to see it.

10. Include links to your Facebook page and Twitter accounts in your e-mail signatures, ensuring that all communication you have acts as a promotion.

11. Enage people with photos. Take pictures that could possibly have a story behind them, and then ask people "What happens next?" and let them add on to a story, creating a growing chain of interest (and spreading the word) at the same time.

Successful Interactions

When you have had a particularly successful social media interaction (the amount varies based on who you ask, but to me when at least 10 people are talking about something I consider this successful) make a record of it for future reference. Do so by taking a screen shot of it and keeping it in your social media strategy guide. If you are unsure of how to do this you could just record a summary (ie: "September 18: Posted about my dog and over 37 people responded"). This helps you look back at what methods were successful to help you think of new ideas that could also be successful.

Chapter 7: Measuring Success

You can do all of the promotion in the world, but if you are not sure what effect it is having, how can you learn from it? The answer is that you can't. That is, not without trying to measure your success.

<u>First Steps</u>

The easiest way to measure success is to start a spreadsheet showing the number of followers (or 'Likes') that you have and the date. Having a yardstick to measure against is always a good thing. It might look something like this:

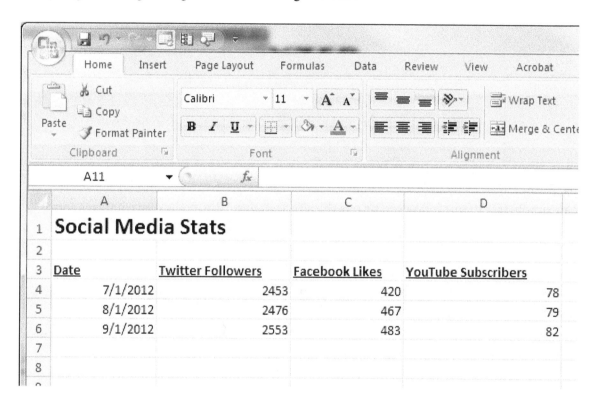

Although this might seem like an extra step of work, it can be very useful in telling you how on track you are in terms of building a social media following. It will also give you guidance on what areas to work on. In the above example, it is easy to see from the numbers that there is growth in the Twitter followers but very little growth with YouTube channel subscribers. Facebook growth is fairly even. These are limited numbers, but it's easy to visually examine a larger set of numbers by creating a graph. The following line chart graph shows that the YouTube growth has flatlined, indicating a possible area to focus on for the following month.

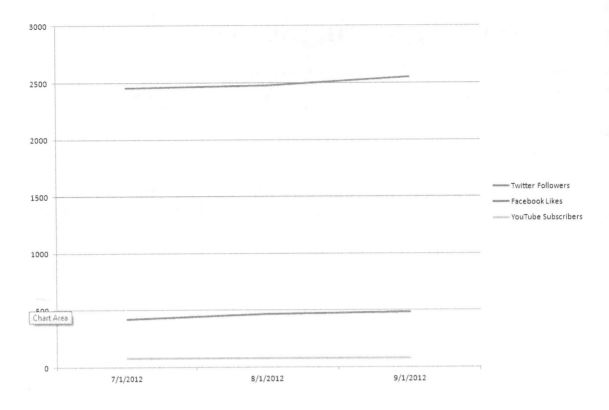

Facebook offers tools such as "Insights" (as described in Chapter 2) and with Twitter you can simply track your followers, or use the site Twitalyzer (http://www.twitalyzer.com).

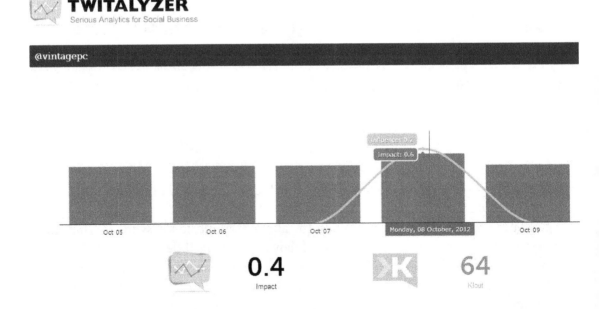

Notice the peak as a tweet was posted. Compare this to others to determine which of your tweets have the most impact.

On Google Plus, there is actually a special place you can go to get information on how the site is working for you. Simply go to http://www.google.com/+/business/measure.html.

With YouTube, the easiest way to measure your success is based on how many people watch your videos, comment, and how many channel subscribers you get.

Website Tracking

All of your social media accounts should point people back to your website especially if this is where they will find contact information and possibly e-commerce options. Tracking your website hits is critical in understanding how successful you are.

There are several ways to do this. Some web hosting companies offer statistics either free or as part of a deluxe package. There are two free options that you can implement that don't require tremendous work to implement.

StatCounter

StatCounter.com is a very early hit tracking website (and one I personally use a lot). Setting up an account and projects (websites) is absolutely free. The system gives you full details of the last 500 visitors per project and if you want more, you can choose to pay for them. You never lose how many people hit your site (even if it is very busy), the free model just retains the full details (location, web browser, etc.) on those last 500 hits.

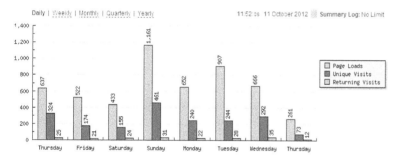

StatCounter will show you the total page loads, unique visitors, and returning visitors as well. When you want more details, it will give you information such as the keywords used to find your page(s) and the websites that linked to your pages.

StatCounter can also give you very useful information such as Screen Resolution Stats. This tells you what screen types your visitors are using, which can be used with your webmaster to determine the size and look of your page. Different websites will have different visitors, and this information be very useful to you.

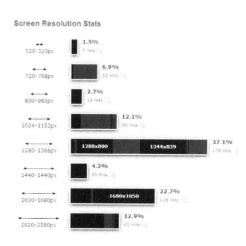

Google Analytics

Google offers its own statistical tracking (analytics.google.com) and is absolutely free. It has very in-depth tracking and even calculates something called the bounce rate (which tracks how many visitors hit a single page on your site and then 'bounce' off to somewhere else).

Analytics also shows you in graph form where your hits are coming from. In this example you can see that fully half the visitors are coming from searches they are doing. Roughly another 25% come from referrals (links on other websites) and the remaining 25% comes from direct traffic.

These numbers are all valuable in determining the direction you will go in for marketing your site and will help you understand better how people find you.

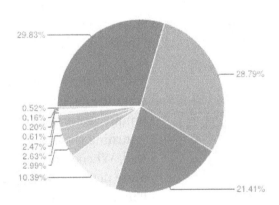

Analytics can also show you what breakdown by browser your site is getting. This will be important because you will want to make sure that when you make any major redesign changes to your site that you have tested it in all the browsers that your visitors are using. Some of the numbers you get back just might surprise you.

Testing sites on various browsers is probably most people's weakness. It's just something that we don't always remember to do.

Summary

Tracking your statistics can become addictive. Measuring yourself against others can bring about its own problems, but at the end of the day it is important to use this information in ways that help you understand your customer. Understanding your customer (and making adjustments accordingly) will definitely result in increased sales.

Chapter 8: Conclusion

It is relatively easy to get your business online with social media. Doing it correctly and effectively, however, is a different story.

It is important to remember that social media is not something that you can just wave your wand at and make work. While joining Facebook and Twitter is free, there is a cost in the amount of time and effort that you will put in to using it. The old saying of the more you put in the more you get it of course applies here as well. Free means it's accessible to everyone. Success? That's a little tougher to come by.

The good news is that there are success stories everywhere. You can enjoy that success just as much as anyone else. All it takes is a little creativity, a lot of work, and a small helping of luck and you will be on your way.

Make sure you create your Social Media Strategy document and refer to it. Change it. Make it a living document. You never know, it might not be long before you are teaching others about what you have learned. In the end, that's really what social media is all about anyways. Pass it on.